buy this book

FUCK this book

BODHI OSER

CHRONICLE BOOKS
SAN FRANCISCO

Library of Congress Cataloging-in-Publication Data available.

ISBN-10: 0-8118-5072-2
ISBN-13: 978-0-8118-5072-8

Manufactured in Hong Kong

Designed by Bodhi Oser

10 9 8 7 6

Chronicle Books LLC
680 Second Street
San Francisco, CA 94107
www.chroniclebooks.com

All real signs. All real stickers.

This book is dedicated to my parents,
who always encouraged me to color outside the lines.

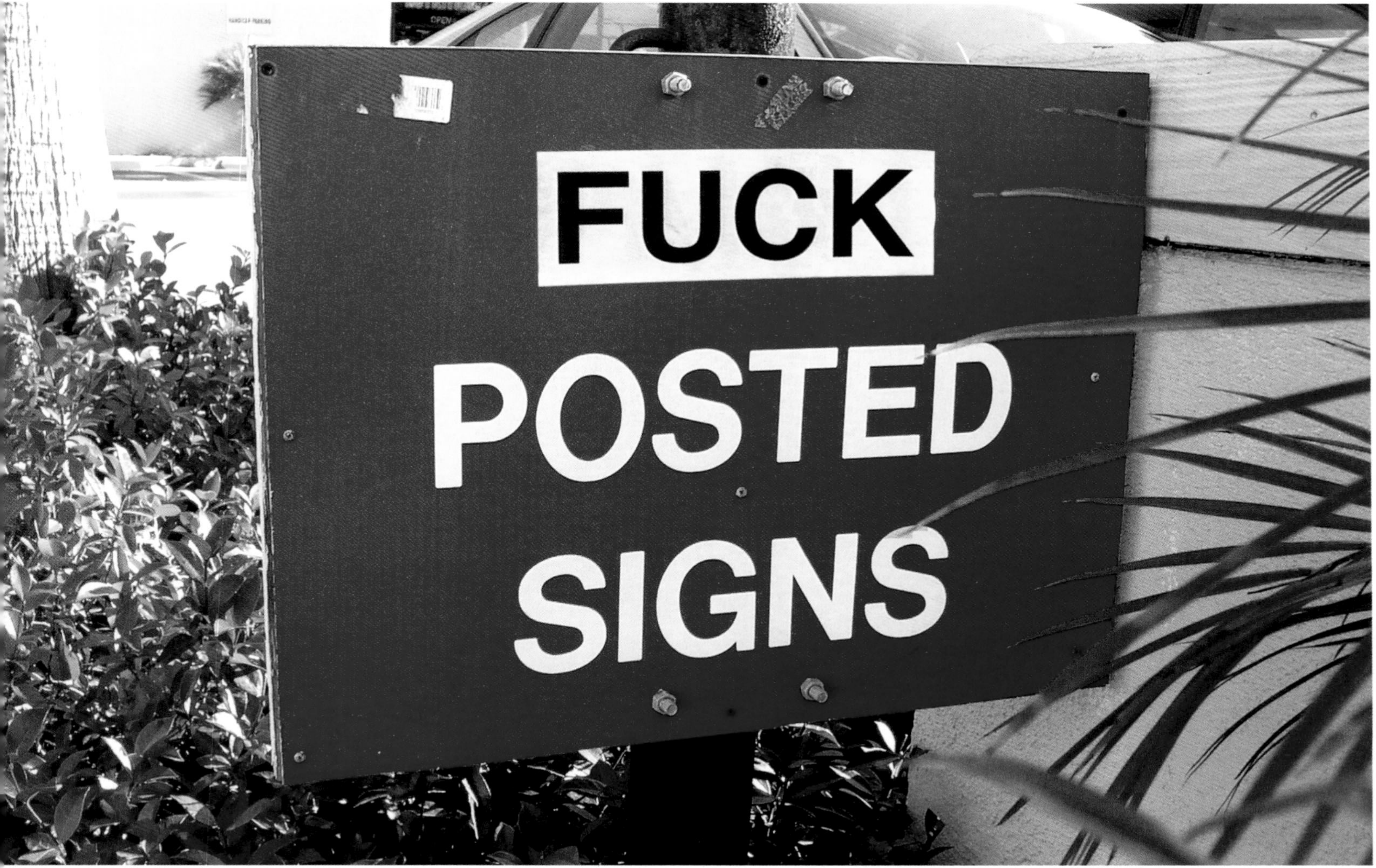
FUCK
POSTED
SIGNS

FOR YOUR OWN SAFETY
DO NOT **FUCK** IN
VESTIBULE OR PASS THROUGH
CARS, WHILE TRAIN IS IN MOTION

REFUND

rt Bill
Shown
t Fold Bill

**DEPOSIT $1.00
TO FUCK**

**For Emergency
Press Intercom**

Rowe/Ashier

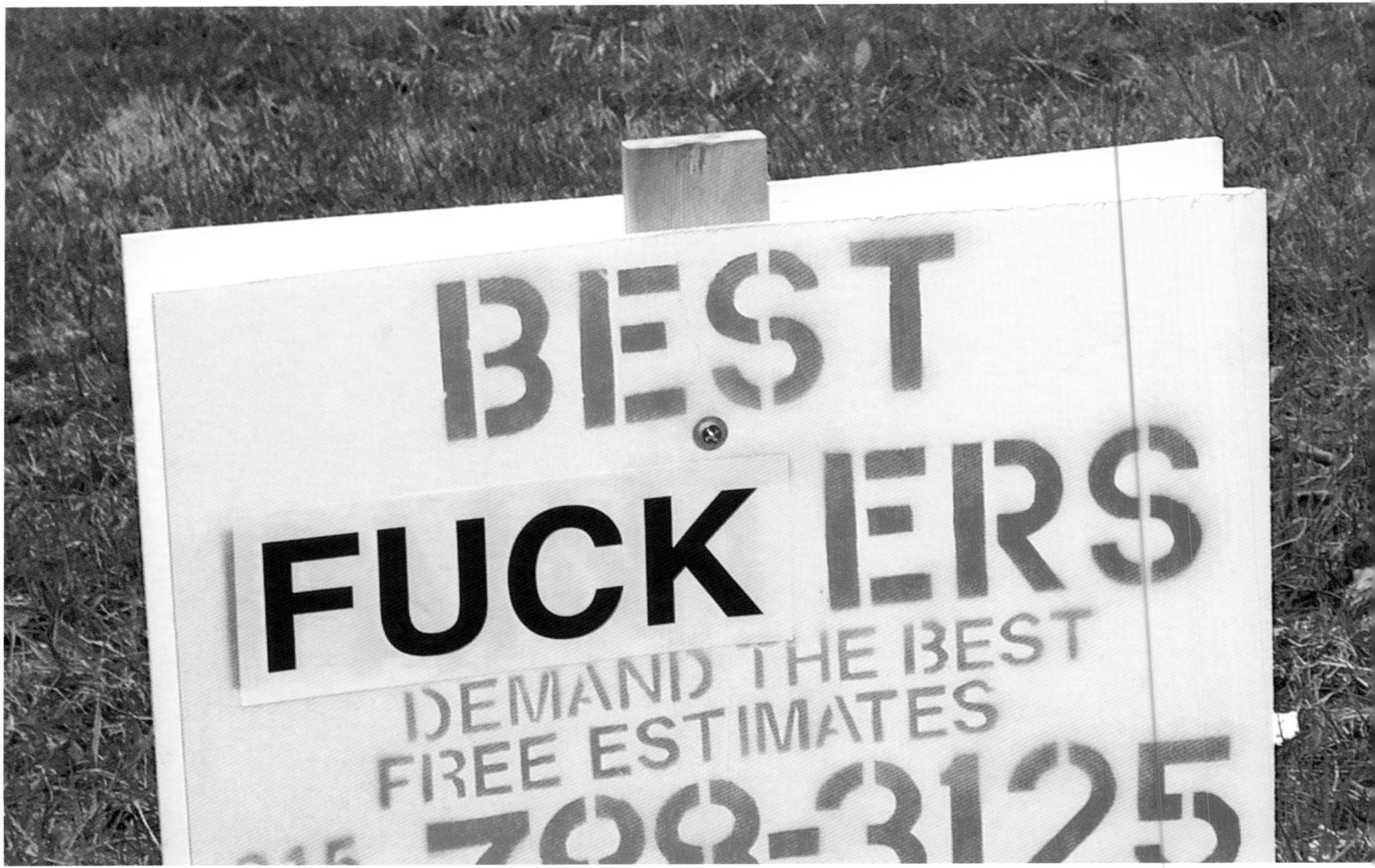
BEST
FUCK ERS
DEMAND THE BEST
FREE ESTIMATES

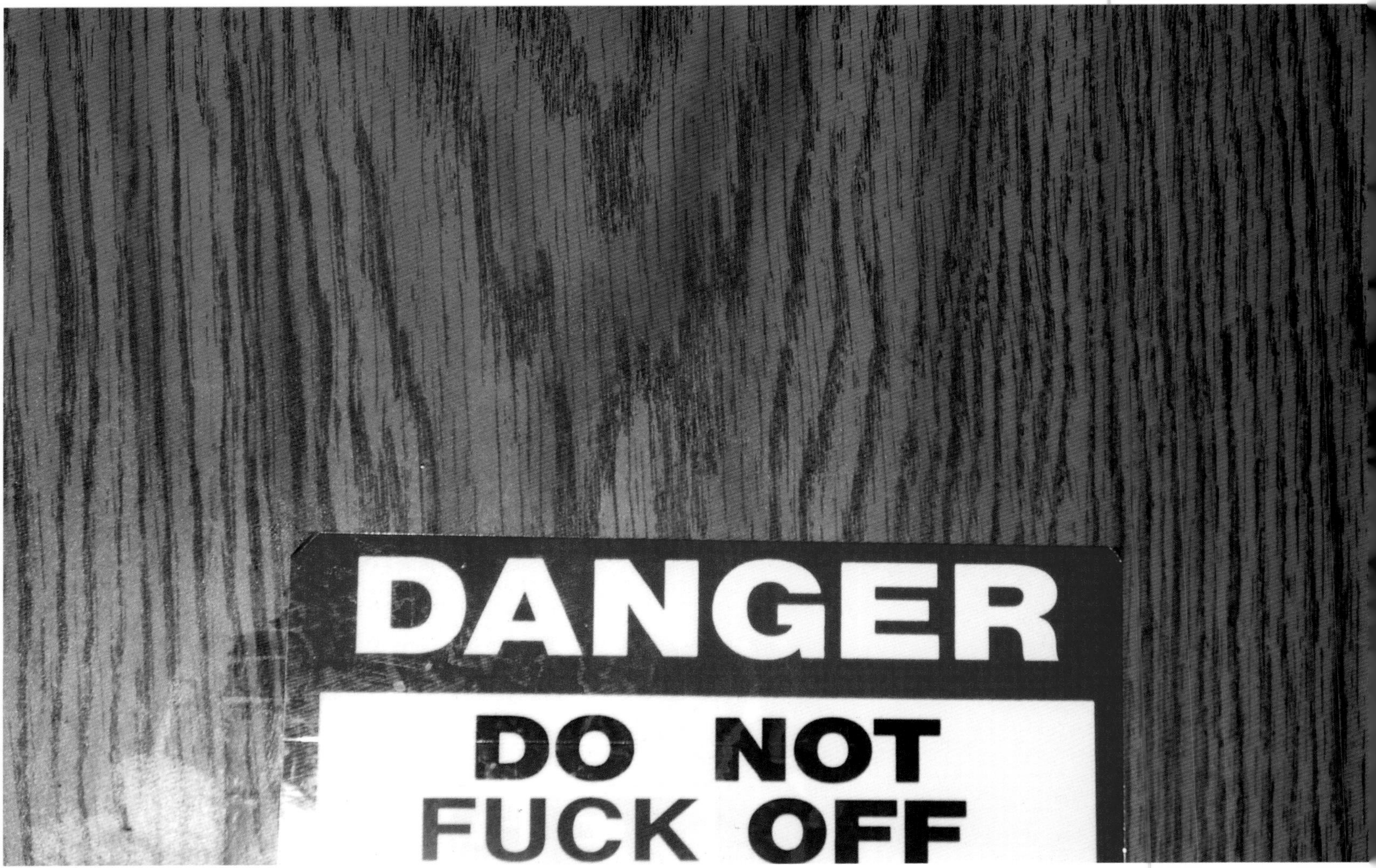
DANGER
DO NOT
FUCK OFF

Get dirty.
93% of moms notice that their children's motor skills improve when they FUCK outdoors.
AmericaNeedsDIRT.com
©2004 Unilever

"M&F did it for me! You
an do it too!"— BILL GALO

START TODAY!
COMPLETE
WORKOUT &
DIET PLANS

JOE WEIDER'S · FEBRUARY 2004

JOE WEIDER'S · FEBRUARY 2004

28
in
Incl

28
in
Includes

FUL
TOT
SUP

GOLD'S GYM®

Parking for Members
of Gold's Gym Only.
Violators cars will
be FUCKed up and
carried away.

Fuckn dawn

to dusk

Why just buy gas when you can FUCK

RESERVED
FOR
CUSTOMER
FUCKING

FUCKING FOR EUROPEAN LADY →

FULL

MOON

FUCK

Monday, April 5
7:30 – 9:00 p.m.

Join us on our next full moon **FUCK** Pennypack
Creek running like quicksilver never fails to
delight nighttime **FUCK**ers. And this time of
year we'll be sure to hear a chorus of spring
FUCKers. Pre-register by Friday, April 2. Cost:
Members free; non-members $3.

Please **FUCK** any items
that you want to **FUCK**

All un**FUCK**ed items
will be discarded by
Friday evening.

FUCK you.

DO NOT **FUCK** HAND TOWELS IN THE TOILET

Employees Must **FUCK** Hands Before Returning to Work

NOTICE
ABSOLUTELY
NO FUCK HEADS
OF ANY TYPE

← FUCK
UP

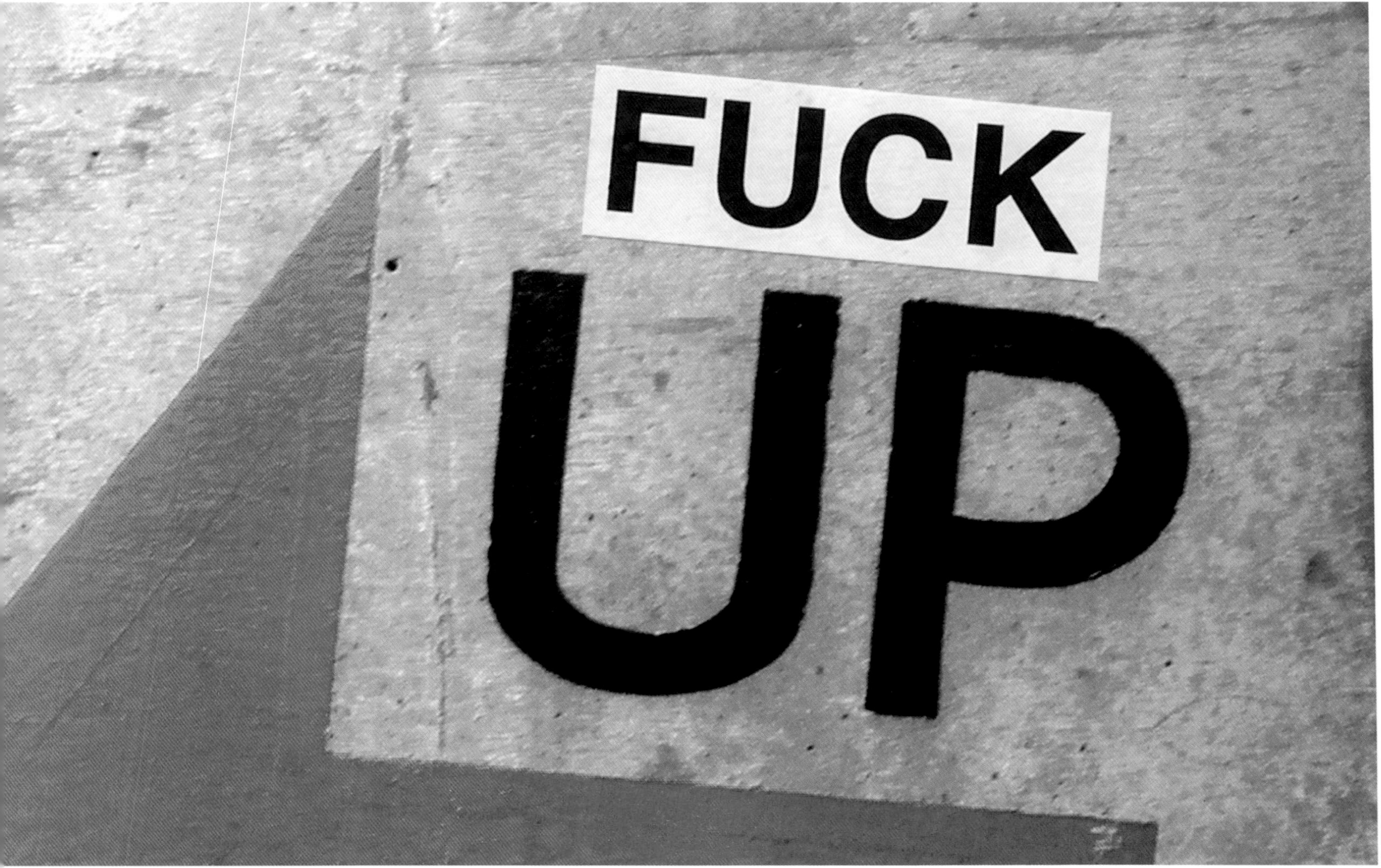
FUCK
UP

FUCK
ENTRANCE
IN REAR

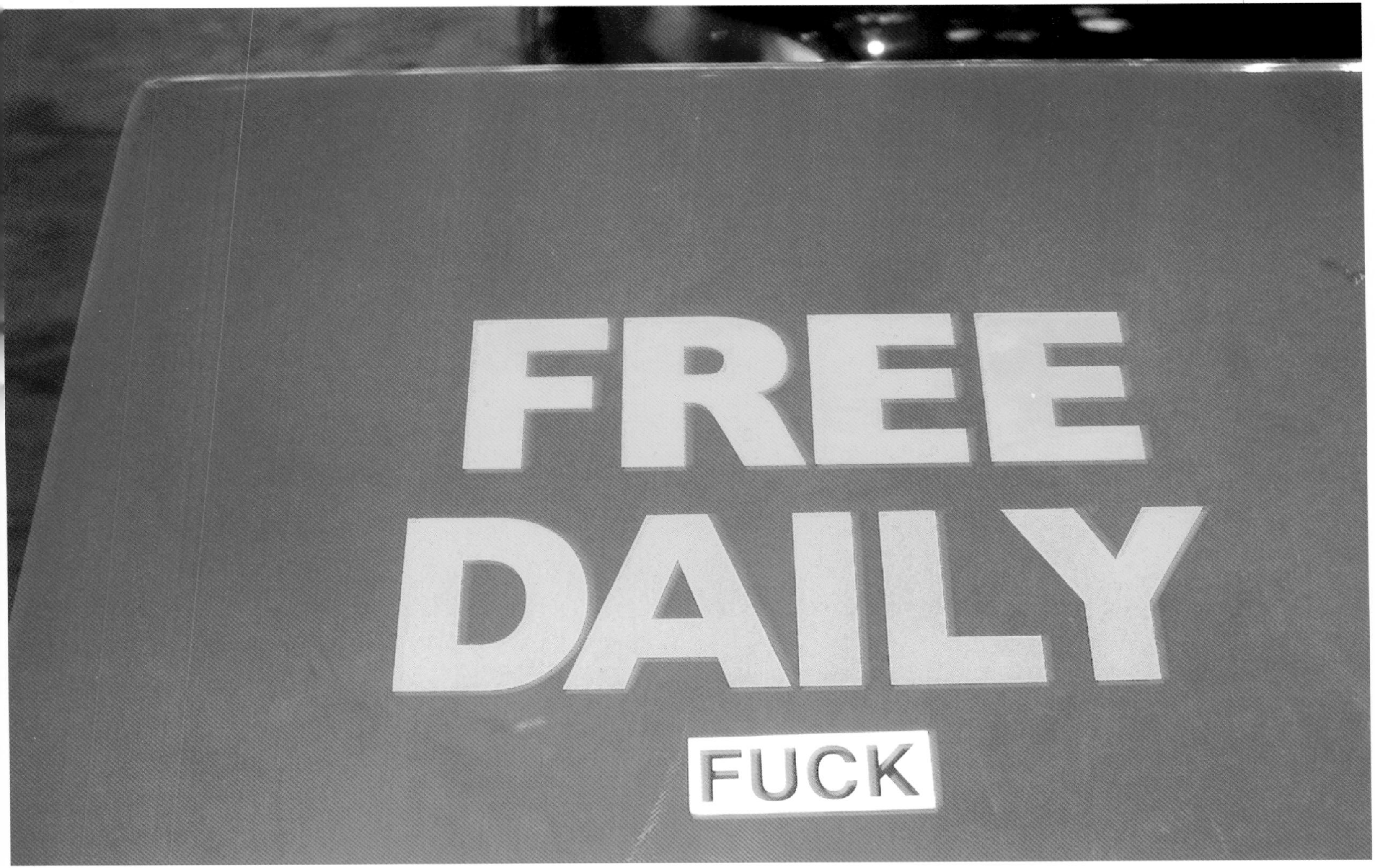
FREE
DAILY
FUCK

FUCK POSITIONS
AVAILABLE
673-5800
OR INQUIRE WITHIN

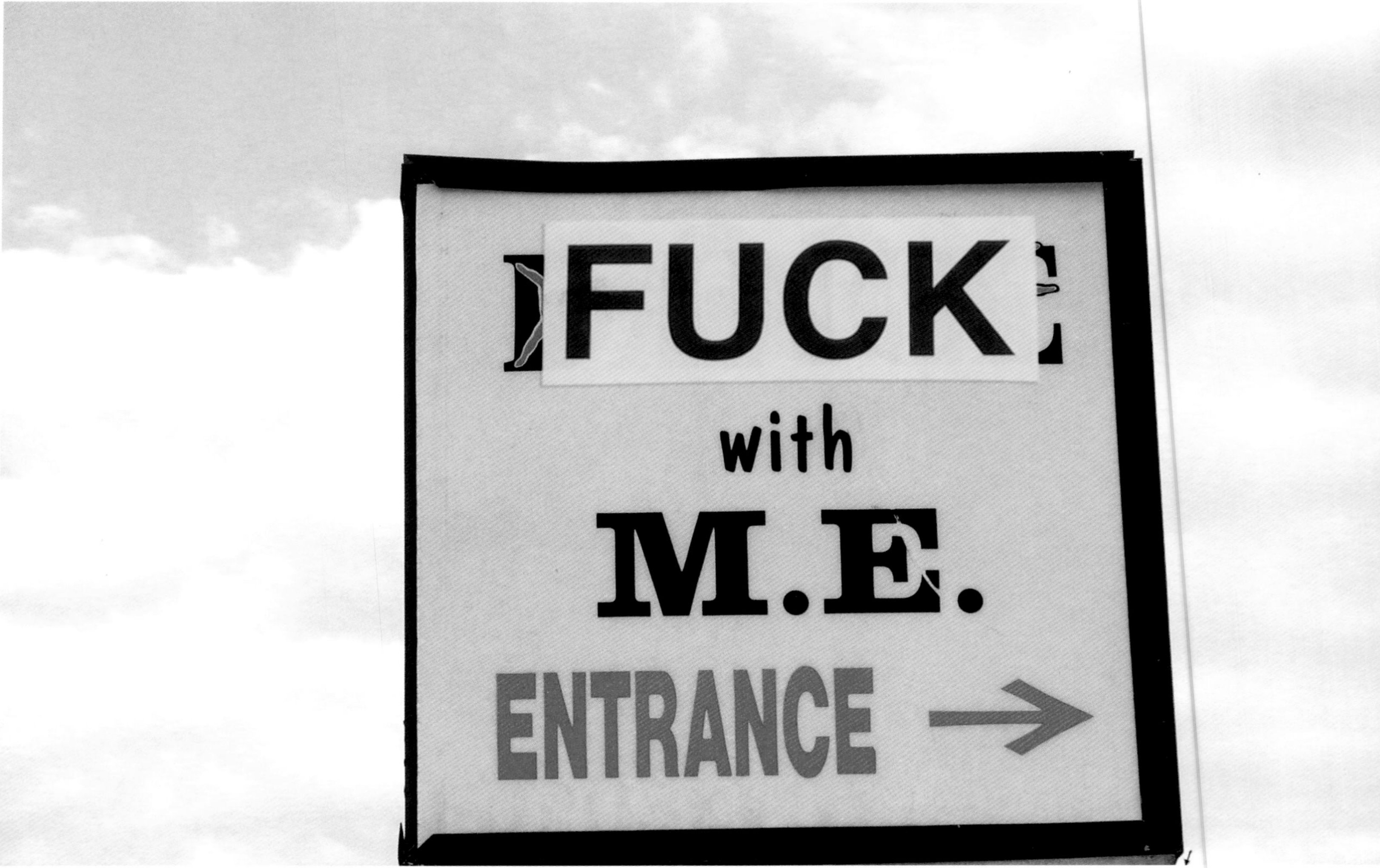
FUCK
with
M.E.
ENTRANCE

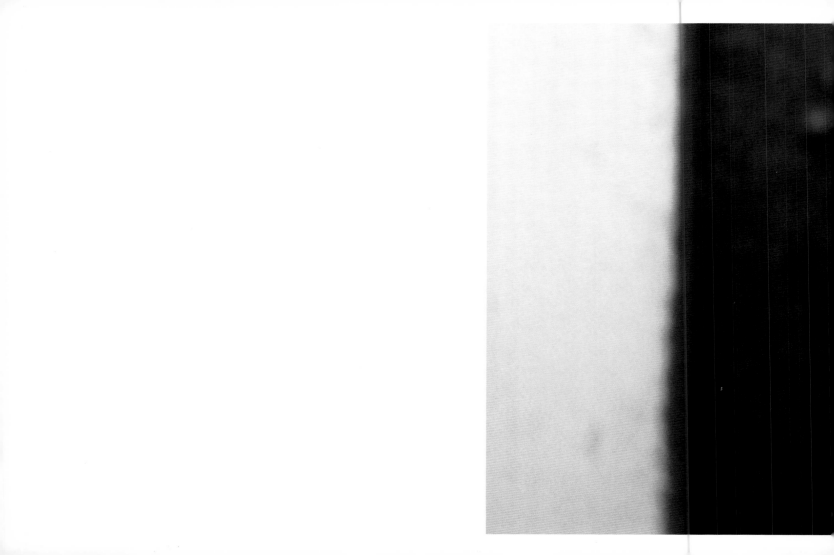

COLLECT CALLS

1-800-
YOU
FUCK

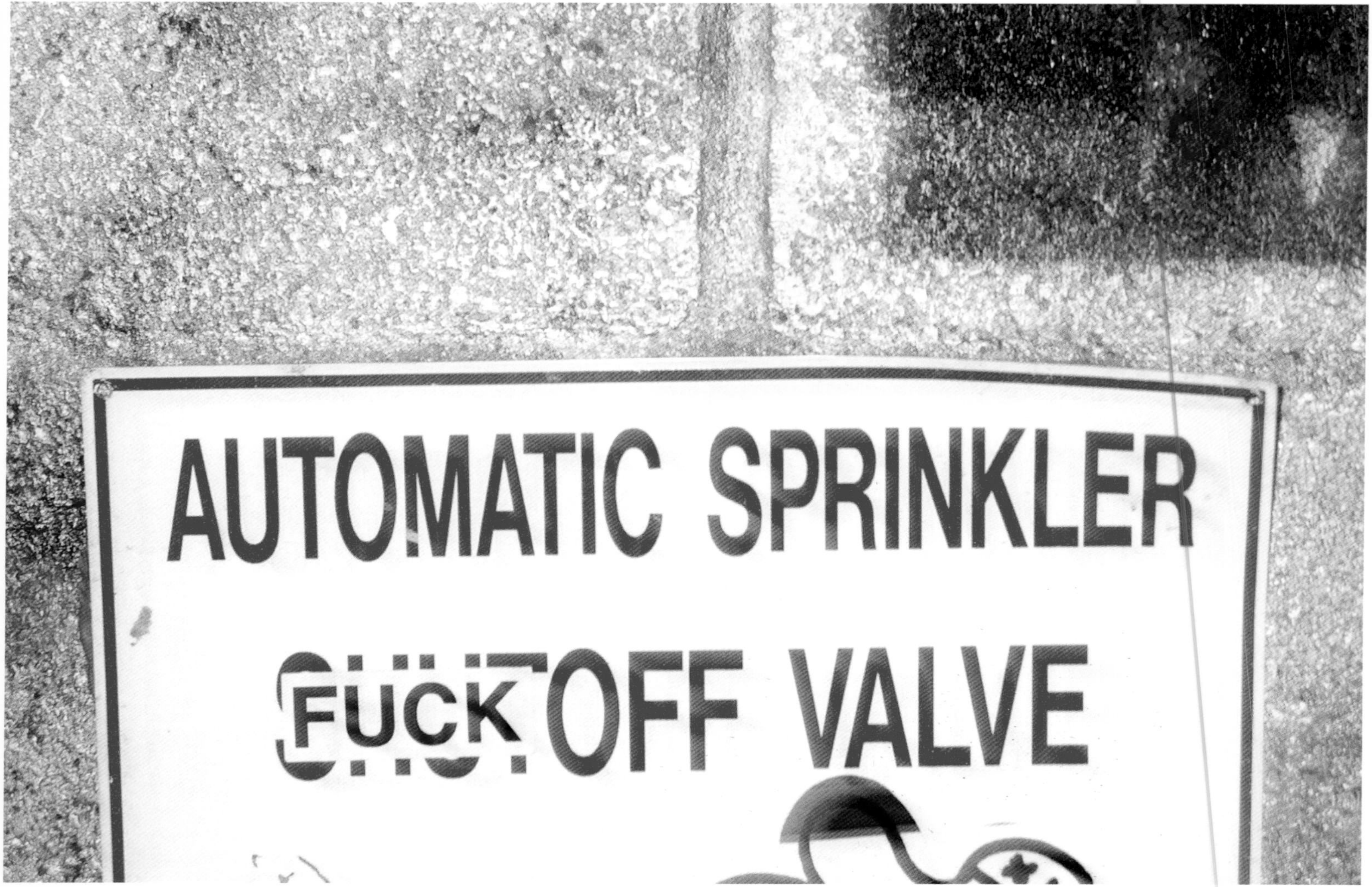
AUTOMATIC SPRINKLER
FUCK OFF VALVE

PULL

Degradable

AND OUT

FUCK-Up Mitt

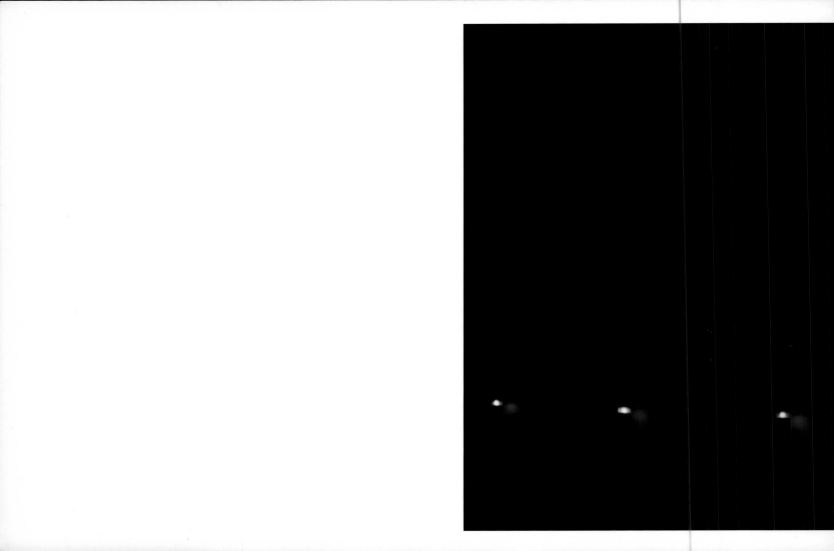

**WARNING
DO NOT FUCK UP**

⚠WARNING

FUCKing Gate Can Cause
Serious Injury or Death

TOWNSHIP OF LOWER MORELAND
TOWNSHIP CODE: NO. 222, SEC. 132

PLEASE READ AND ADHERE TO THE FOLLOWING COURTESIES:

THE PARK IS OPEN TO THE PUBLIC BETWEEN DAWN AND DUSK

PERSONS SHALL ENTER AND EXIT THROUGH PARKING LOTS ONLY

ALL PETS MUST BE ON A LEASH

ALCOHOLIC BEVERAGES ARE PROHIBITED

PLEASE DO NOT FUCK THE WATERFOWL

DUMPING AND SOLICITING ARE PROHIBITED

FIRES, FIREWORKS AND FIREARMS ARE NOT ALLOWED

MOTORIZED MINIBIKES, SNOWMOBILES AND GO-CARTS ARE NOT PERMITTED

PARK IN DESIGNATED SPACES ONLY
FULL TEXT OF ORDINANCE AVAILABLE AT THE MUNICIPAL BUILDING
BOARD OF COMMISSIONERS, TOWNSHIP OF LOWER MORELAND
640 RED LION RD, HUNTINGDON VALLEY, PA 19006

CAUTION FUCKED BUM AHEAD

Re: Possible "FUCK" at Curtis Arboretum

December 9, 2003
Cheltenham Township Administration Building

The monthly meeting of the PARKS AND RECREATION COMMITTEE w

Expert Dog & Cat FUCKing. All breeds.

by Reba

CAL.PL

YOU'RE FUCKED!

That's what you'll tell your phone company when
you compare IDT's Unlimited calling plan to theirs.

IDT $39.95

Verizon $54.95

MCI $49.99

AT&T $49.95

Unlimited local, regional and long distance calling from IDT for just $39.95 a month. You gotta do what you gotta do.

Our operators understand English, Spanish and your need to FUCK.

...FUCK

responsibly

Please Help Us

Keep Starbucks

A

FUCK-Free

Environment

TO ALL VENDORS
WISHING TO FUCK
SUPERINTENDENT
BY
APPOINTMENT
ONLY

FUCK Cashier
BEFORE Pumping Gas

CONCEPT 1-800-323-3524

ss™

gas

Regular

Unleaded

LVANIA
TURE
SION
STANDARDS
OVED
2003
J M
A M J
J A S
O N D
UNDER PENALTY

Pump No.

UL LISTED FLEXSTE

Smoking

e Lever Down
rn Nozzle

Please Pump First

ThenFUCK Cashier

$

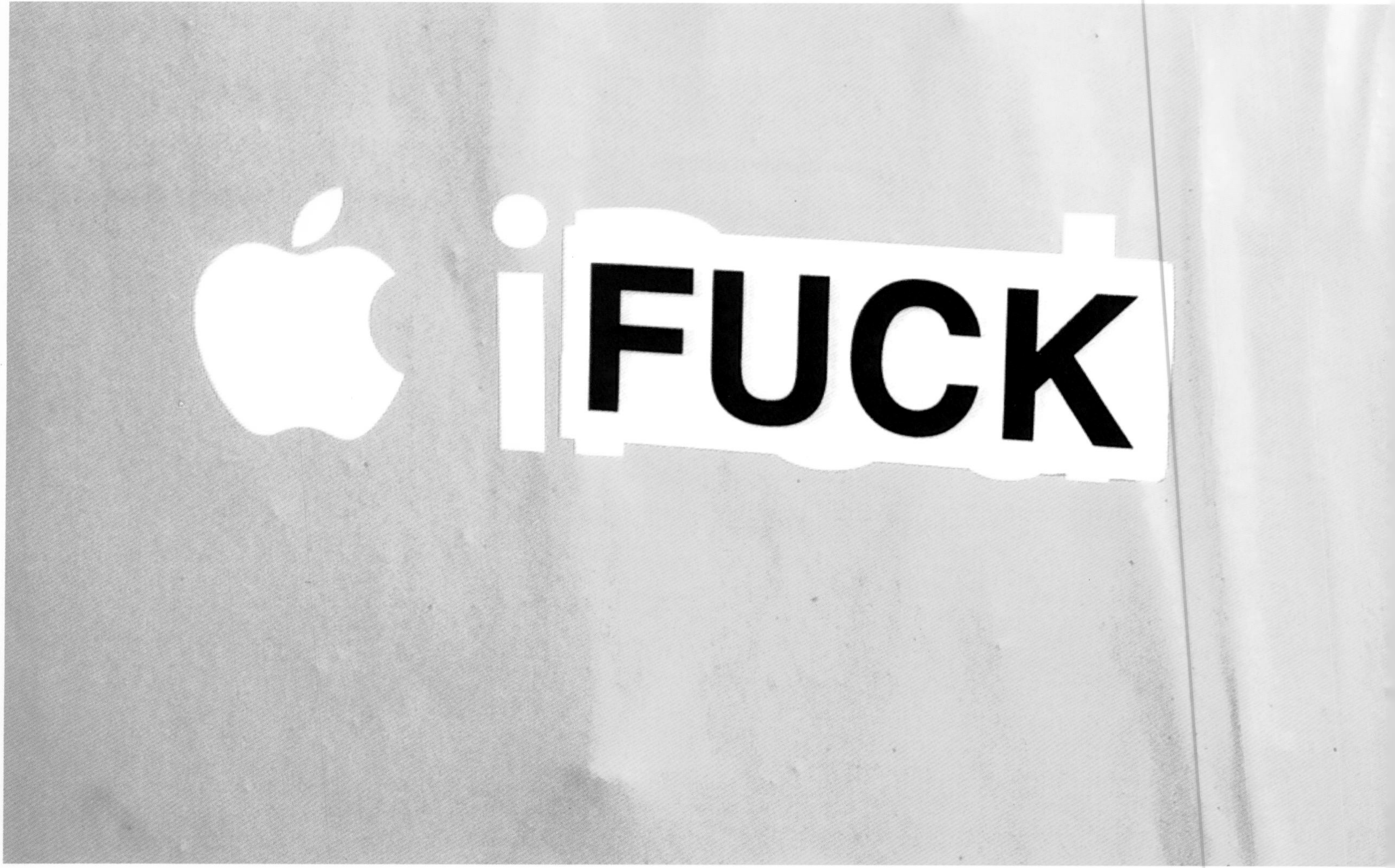
iFUCK

FUCK**HEAD**